Easy Bible Object Talks

by Larry R. Michaels

illustrated by
Timothy A. Heck

STANDARD PUBLISHING
Cincinnati, Ohio

Sharing the thoughts of his own heart, the author may express views that are not entirely consistent with those of the publisher.

ISBN 0-87239-846-3

Copyright © 1985. The STANDARD PUBLISHING Company, Cincinnati, Ohio
A division of STANDEX INTERNATIONAL Corporation. Printed in U.S.A.

Contents

Preface

Teaching with object talks is one of the best ways to make a lasting impression on your students. And it is perhaps the most versatile method of teaching available. Use it in Sunday school, Vacation Bible School, or Youth hour. Use it for a devotional at a party or social. Use it wherever and whenever you wish.

Because it is so easy to teach with object talks, they can be used to help a young person or a new teacher present his first lesson. They make great emergency lessons when a teacher gets sick at the last minute and a substitute has no time to prepare, too.

We hope you will enjoy these object talks. We present them with the hope that they will be a blessing to you and your students.

ARITHMETIC BOOK

NEED: An arithmetic book and a Bible.
TEXT: 2 Timothy 3:14-17.
POINT: We read the Bible to learn about God.

How many of you go to school? Do you learn arithmetic in school? Let's see how you are doing in arithmetic. What is 2 + 2? What is 9 − 5? I can see that you have learned your arithmetic very well.

How did you learn to do arithmetic so well? Do you have a book at school to help you? Maybe it is a book something like this. *(Show the arithmetic book.)* In an arithmetic book, there are sample problems and explanations showing you how to add and subtract. Suppose you wanted to learn about fractions. Where would you look? You'd look in an arithmetic book like this, wouldn't you? An arithmetic book can come in handy when you need to know about numbers. Now I want to show you another book I brought with me today.

What book can you read to learn about God? *(Show the Bible.)* Just as you use an arithmetic book to learn about adding and subtracting, you look in the Bible to learn about God. Does the Bible tell us about Jesus? Does it tell us about God's love and forgiveness? Does it tell us about what God's people have done? It tells us about all those things, doesn't it? The Bible shows us what God is like, and what He wants us to do. It's a very important book. When we want to know something about God, we have to know where to look.

If you wanted to learn how to add, would you look in a reading book? Would you look in a cookbook? No, because you wouldn't find what you were looking for, would you? In the same way, you wouldn't learn about God in this arithmetic book. You learn about God in this other book, the Bible.

Summary: It's a good thing we have books to help us learn, isn't it? But we have to know what books to use. The Bible is a very special book, because it teaches us about God. That's the reason the Bible is such an important book. It tells us what we need to know about God. To learn how to add and subtract, we use an arithmetic book. But we read the Bible to learn about God.

BASKETBALL PRACTICE

NEED: A basketball.
TEXT: Luke 18:1.
POINT: As disciples of Jesus, we practice living the way He taught us to live.

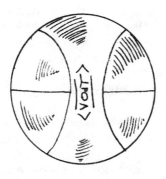

Does everyone know what I brought with me today? (*A basketball.*) How many of you like to play basketball? If you've ever tried to play basketball, you know that making a basket is not very easy, especially at first. The rim is only a few inches larger than the basketball; so you have to shoot the ball just right to get it through the basket.

What do you have to do to be a good basketball player? Are you good at shooting baskets the first time you try? No, you have to practice, don't you? The more you practice, the better you get. Now let me ask you another question:

Why do you think Jesus said to pray always and not give up? Did He mean that we have to pray often to get God's attention? Do we have to repeat ourselves so that God will listen to us? No, of course not. When Jesus told His disciples to pray always, He wanted them to be able to understand God's will for them better. In that way, praying is something like practicing basketball. The more we go to God in prayer, the better we understand what He wants us to do.

Do you become a good basketball player just for your own benefit? No, you don't play a basketball game by yourself, do you? You try to help the whole team. In a basketball game, each member of the team tries his best to help the whole team win. In the same way, God wants us to be members of His team. He wants us to work together as His people, the church, to be His disciples in the world. That's the reason He wants us to get to know His will better through prayer, so we can be better members of His team. Also, He doesn't want us to lose heart.

What happens when a team loses a game? Do all the players quit and say, "I'm never going to play basketball again"? No, they go back to practice, don't they? They begin preparing for the next game. Sometimes in life, too, things go wrong, and bad things happen to us. Should we just give up and quit? No, God tells us to turn to Him in prayer with our problems and not give up. That's one reason Jesus tells us as His disciples to pray always and not lose heart.

Summary: The next time you try to shoot a basket, remember that it takes practice to become a good basketball player. In the same way, Jesus tells us to practice turning to God in prayer so that we can become better at knowing His will and helping His team. Also, Jesus wants us never to lose heart. No matter what happens to us in life, we know that we can always take it to God in prayer.

BINOCULARS

NEED: A pair of binoculars.
TEXT: Luke 1:46.
POINT: God wants us to make Him big in our lives and with our lives.

What do I have with me today? (*A pair of binoculars.*) What do you use binoculars for? They help you to see things that are far away, don't they? They make things that are far away seem very close. Binoculars have lenses in them that *magnify* what you are looking at. When something is magnified thirty-five or fifty times, it looks bigger and closer.

Have any of you ever used binoculars? Where did you use them? *(At a ballgame, a concert, etc.)* At a baseball game, for example, binoculars let you see the players "up close." You can watch the catcher give the pitcher his signals or even see the expressions on the players' faces. Binoculars make everything look bigger. They magnify everything you look at.

Who would like to look through these binoculars today? (*Let a child look through them.*) Did everything look bigger and closer to you? That's because everything you see is magnified. In the Bible, Mary said, "My soul magnifies the Lord." She was thankful that she would give birth to the baby Jesus. She meant that God was very big and close to her. She saw God as if she were looking through binoculars.

Is God close to us? Sure! He is always right here with us, isn't He? Is God really big in our lives? Yes, He is the most important thing in our lives. God wants us to realize His importance and to see Him as big and close to us. He wants us to magnify Him in everything we do, and to make Him the biggest thing in our lives.

Have you ever looked through binoculars from the wrong end? How does everything look then? (*Let someone try it.*) Everything looks small and far away, doesn't it? Some people see God as if they were looking through the wrong end of binoculars. They try to keep Him far away and not let Him be part of their lives. But we can't keep God away from us, can we? He is always with us.

How do we magnify God in our lives? He tells us to praise Him, to give Him thanks for all He has given us, to read about Him in the Bible, and to do the things He wants us to do. These are just some ways that we can make God big in our lives. That's what it means to magnify the Lord.

Summary: We can't see God through binoculars, can we? But we can magnify God in our lives. The next time you look at something through binoculars, remember that nothing is bigger or closer to us than God.

CAMPAIGNING FOR GOD

NEED: Campaign poster, button, or sign.
TEXT: 2 Corinthians 1:20.
POINT: God want us to tell others that He keeps His promises.

Who can tell me how someone gets to be President of the United States? That person has to get the most votes and win an election, doesn't he? But before a person can be elected, he has to *campaign*. That means he tells everyone what he will do if people vote for him. Suppose you wanted to be elected to something, perhaps president of your class.

How would you get people to vote for you? You might tell people how well qualified you are. You might tell them what you would do if you were elected. And you might ask your friends to tell other people about you. All these things are called campaigning. It's the same thing a person does if he wants to be elected President of the United States.

Have you ever seen a sign like this before? It's a campaign poster. It tells you about a person who wants your vote.

People who want this person elected might give you one of these. They want to tell you about their candidate. The Bible tells us that we should do the same thing for God. He wants us to campaign for Him. But instead of getting people to vote for Him, He wants people to trust Him and follow Him.

Can you think of anyone we can trust more than God? He is certainly well qualified, isn't He? He is worthy of our trust. He not only made us, but He loves us, protects us, and promises to be with us forever. Sometimes people who want us to vote for them make promises that they can't keep. But God keeps every promise, doesn't He? In the Bible, God kept every promise He made to His people. We can trust Him completely. Since we believe that God is worthy of our trust, He wants us to tell others about Him. We don't have to carry campaign posters, but we can tell other people all the things God has done for us in our lives and how much we trust in His promises.

Summary: In the next election, ask your parents how they decided whom to vote for. Maybe they saw a campaign poster like this. Just as people who want to be elected ask their friends to campaign for them, God wants us to campaign for Him. He wants us to tell other people that He always keeps His promises.

CHOSEN FOR GOD'S TEAM

NEED: A baseball bat.
TEXT: 1 Peter 2:9, 10.
POINT: God has chosen us to be members of His team, to be His special people.

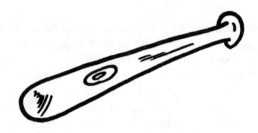

Does everyone know what I have with me today? (*A baseball bat*.) How many of you like to play baseball? Then I'm sure you know what you use a baseball bat for. Baseball wouldn't be much fun without a bat to hit the ball, would it? Sometimes there's another thing you use a baseball bat for. You do this before the game even begins. Suppose you have all your friends together for a game and you've picked a captain for each team.

Does anyone know what you do next before the game begins? (*Choose up sides.*) When you begin to choose up sides, how do you decide which team picks first? Let's try it now. Will someone volunteer to be a team captain with me? (*Pick a volunteer.*) Let's pretend that you and I are going to pick teams. Who gets to pick first? To decide, you toss the bat to me. Then we put our hands on top of each other's hands like this. Whoever comes out on top picks first, right? Then we begin to choose teams. We all want to be chosen on a team, don't we? Let me ask you another question:

Do you think God wants us to be members of His team? The Bible tells us that we are God's chosen people. He has chosen us to be on His team. In other words, He wants us to work together with all the other people He has chosen to do His work here in His world. The church is like God's team. We are all members who work together to do what God wants us to do. You and I and all of us work together as a team.

Does every member of a baseball team have to work together in order to win the game? Suppose everyone on your team was trying to win but the shortstop. Every time a ground ball came to him, he wouldn't catch it. You probably wouldn't win the game, would you? God has chosen each of us to be on His team so that we can all work together for Him in His church. Besides that, just as it is fun to play baseball, God wants us to enjoy being on His team.

Have you ever felt left out when teams were chosen? Many times smaller children get left out of ball games. The big kids choose teams, and no one wants little kids on his team. The smaller children have to sit there and watch, because no one chooses them. Have you ever felt that way?

Is God like those big kids, too? No! He chose each one of us. It doesn't matter how big we are or how good we are, because we are all special to Him. He loves each of us. Through His Son, Jesus, He has chosen us to be on His own team. All He asks is that we try our very best to do what He wants us to do to help His team.

Summary: The next time you play baseball and choose up teams, remember that the Bible tells us that God has chosen each of us to be a member of His own special team forever.

DIARY

NEED: A diary and a Bible.
TEXT: 1 Corinthians 10:11.
POINT: We see God's actions clearly in the things He has done for His people throughout history, especially in Jesus Christ.

How many of you know what a diary is? I brought a diary with me today to show you. You can see that it is a book that you write in. *(Show the diary.)* It has a different page for each day, and you can write down the things you did and thought about that day. Then later you can look back and remember what you did. Have any of you ever written in a diary like this?

What kind of things would you write in your diary? You might write today that you went to church. You might write about what you learned in Sunday school. You might write down the names of your friends and your teachers. Then someday, maybe years from now, you can look at your diary and remember all the things you did today and the people you did them with. Let me ask you another question:

19

Do you think God keeps a diary? What book do I have in my hand? *(Show the Bible.)* The Bible could be called God's diary. I say that because the Bible is a record of things God has done for His people throughout history. For example, we can read in the Bible about how God created the world and everything in it. We can read about Abraham and Moses and David, and how God kept His promises to them. We can read God's words as He spoke through prophets like Isaiah and Jeremiah.

But what do you think is the most important thing God did? He sent His Son, Jesus, to us, didn't He? Is that written down in the Bible? Yes, the Bible tells us all about Jesus. In fact, the Bible has four accounts, or diaries, about Him. They are called *Gospels*. They tell us the good news about Jesus' life and teachings. We can read about all the works He did. We can also read about His death on the cross and His resurrection from the dead. It's all written down in the Bible.

Why is it important to read about God in the Bible? Do we know that God loves us? Yes, because we can read about God's love in the Bible. Do we know that God forgives us? Yes, because He forgives others like us in the Bible. Do we know we will live with God forever? Yes, because the Bible tells us we will. It's good that we have this written record of God's actions so we can know what God is like. The Bible is like God's diary, because we can read it and remember the things that God has done. Then we can understand all the things He does for us.

Summary: I'm sure many of you will keep a diary like this someday. Then you can look back and remember things you have done. Like a diary, the Bible helps us look back and remember all the things God has done for us.

FISHERS OF MEN

NEED: Two fishing poles: a regular pole and a simple pole made out of a stick with string attached. At the end of the string, have a magnet with a heart pasted on it. Also have some paper-doll people with paper-clips on them in a container.

TEXT: Matthew 4:18-22.

POINT: Jesus calls His followers to become fishers of men.

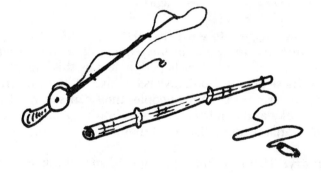

How many of you like to go fishing? Good, then you know what you use to catch fish. You probably use a fishing pole like this one. *(Show the real fishing rod.)* What is on the end of this fishing rod? It has a hook, doesn't it? You would probably put a worm on this hook, and when the fish ate the worm, he would be caught. Then you would reel him in. Did you know that in the Bible, Jesus talks about fishing? Peter, Andrew, James, and John were all fishermen. Those disciples made their living by catching fish. But Jesus told them about a different kind of fishing.

What do you think Jesus meant when He told them, "I will make you fishers of men"? Did He want them to go out and catch people with hooks? No, of course not. Today

I brought with me another fishing pole to show you what Jesus was talking about when He told them to become "fishers of men." This isn't a very fancy fishing pole, is it? What is on the end of this string? *(A heart.)*

Why would we have a heart on the end of our fishing pole? Can we become fishers of people with love? Yes, we can. God tells us that we should love one another because that's the way we show them what God's love is like. We bring people to God by treating them the way God has treated us. Jesus shows us how much God loves us, and He wants us to show others how much He loves them, too. That's what He means when He tells us to become fishers of men. Let's see how that works.

Can we catch people with this fishing pole? *(Reach into the container and pull out the paper-doll people with the magnet.)* God's love attracts people just as this magnet attracts these people. God's love is like that. When we spread His love around to other people, they can see what His love is like and can become His followers. That's the way Jesus wants us to be fishers of men.

Summary: The next time you go fishing, think of these words of Jesus. He wants us to be fishers of men. He doesn't want us to catch people with hooks as we catch fish, but He wants us to catch people with love. Just as Jesus showed us God's love, we can show God's love to others. Then they will want to follow Him, too.

FIVE KERNELS OF CORN

NEED: Five kernels of corn.
TEXT: 1 Thessalonians 5:18.
POINT: God wants us to give thanks for everything He has given us.

How many of you like to eat? What is your favorite food? Is anyone hungry now? It just so happens I brought some food with me. Does this look good to you? *(Show the kernels of corn on a plate.)* Doesn't this make your mouth water? Then let me ask you this:

Do you know who the first settlers were that came to America? They were called the Pilgrims. Do you know what they counted on for food? *(Corn.)* The Indians taught them how to grow corn, and it became their main food. One year, the frost came early, and a large part of the corn crop was destroyed. The Pilgrims were in danger of starving during the long winter. So they divided up the corn they had, and each person got just five kernels a meal. Do you think they were thankful, even for just that little bit? We always picture the first Thanksgiving as a huge feast, but I imagine our early settlers were even *more* thankful for these few kernels of corn. That was all the food they had.

Are you thankful for the food you eat? How about spinach and broccoli? We can be pretty fussy about food sometimes, can't we? Sometimes we're not very thankful. But if you were dying of hunger, you wouldn't refuse a plate of spinach, would you? It's when our plates are always full that we take food for granted, and we sometimes forget to say, "Thank You," to God for all the things He gives us.

Summary: The next time you sit down to a big meal, like at Thanksgiving, remember what the first settlers in America had to eat during that long winter. Yet they gave thanks to God for what they had because it kept them alive. God wants us to give thanks for everything He has given us, even if sometimes it is only five kernels of corn.

GRAIN OF SALT

NEED: A saltshaker.
TEXT: 2 Peter 3:8.
POINT: God's love lasts forever.

Did you ever think that some days would never end?
Maybe you had to go to the dentist. Maybe you were hungry, and it seemed school would never end so you could go home and eat. Or maybe you were sick and had to stay in bed all day, and time went very slowly. But if a day can seem like a long time, can you imagine how long a thousand years can be? No one can ever live that long. A thousand years is a very long time, isn't it? Yet the Bible says that with God a thousand years is like a single day. I brought something today to help us understand what that means.

What do I have in my hand? *(A saltshaker.)* Who can tell me how many grains of salt are in this saltshaker? Are there more than ten? More than one hundred? More than even one thousand? Yes, there are thousands of grains of salt in this shaker, aren't there? Let's pretend that each of these grains of salt is like a day in our lives. *(Shake a few grains*

27

into the palm of your hand.) They look pretty small to us, don't they? But each grain is important. Suppose for a minute you are an ant.

Each grain of salt would look pretty big to an ant, wouldn't it? If an ant was hungry for salt, each grain would be a big bite for him. That's the way time looks to us. Each day seems big to us, but God can see thousands of days all at once. That's why the Bible says that with God a thousand years is like a single day, and a day like a thousand years.

Who can tell me how many days there are in a year? That's right, 365, and 366 in a leap year. So that means a thousand years has 365,250 days. That's a lot of days, isn't it? But the Bible tells us that 365,250 days is the same as one day with God. He is here with us every day. He is with us today, and He will be with people here 365,250 days from now. God is eternal—He is with us forever.

Will there ever be a time when God is not with us? No, because He promises to be with us and to love us forever. Even though there are thousands of grains of salt in this saltshaker, sooner or later, if you salt enough potatoes, they will all be gone. And even all the grains of salt on earth could eventually be used up. But the Bible says that God's presence with us and His love for us never run out. That's the reason we have patience and hope, because God promises He will be with us always, now and forever. He can do that because with God a thousand years is the same as a single day.

Summary: There are thousands of grains of salt in this shaker, and if each one is like a day, they'd add up to a long time. But to God, one day is the same as 365,250 days. We know that He is here with us today, and He will be with us every day—forever.

THE GREAT ERASER

NEED: A chalkboard and an eraser with "JESUS" taped to the back.

TEXT: Mark 2:1-12.

POINT: Jesus has the power to forgive sins.

Does everyone know what this is? *(A chalkboard.)* Those of you who are in school probably know what a chalkboard is used for. Have any of you written on a chalkboard at school? Today I'm going to write on this chalkboard for you. Let's begin with some arithmetic. *(Write 2+2=5.)*

Two plus two equals five, right? No? Did I make a mistake? If I didn't get the right answer, what do I have to use to change it? *(Hold up the eraser.)* Luckily, I brought something with me to erase my wrong answer. *(Erase the five.)* Who knows what the right answer is? *(Write it on the board.)* Let's try writing something else on the blackboard. *(Write, "I hate you.")*

Is that what God wants us to say to one another? No. It looks as if I made another mistake. What should I have written instead? What do I have to do to correct my mistake? *(Erase "hate" and write "love.")* That sounds better, doesn't it?

Is there anyone here who has never made a mistake? We all make mistakes, don't we? Sometimes we do the wrong thing or say the wrong thing. There's a word for that in the Bible. It's called *sin.* Sin is something we do to hurt someone or something we say to make another person feel badly. Or sometimes it's not doing something to help someone. Sin is doing the wrong thing or not doing the right thing, like my mistakes here on the blackboard. Did you ever feel sorry you made a mistake, but didn't know what to do about it?

What does God do about our mistakes? He did something very special. He doesn't want anything to keep us apart from Him; so He did something to correct our mistakes. God sent someone to us to bring His forgiveness into the world so that our mistakes, or our sins, could be erased.

Does anyone know who came to forgive our sins? *(Jesus.)* The Bible tells us that Jesus is like this eraser. *(Show His name on the eraser.)* Just as this eraser wiped my mistakes off this chalkboard, Jesus, the Son of God, is able to wipe away all our mistakes in God's eyes. Then, just as we corrected our mistakes, we can begin again to try to do the right things that God wants us to do.

Summary: The next time you make a mistake and reach for an eraser, remember that Jesus is like this eraser because He has the power to wipe our sins away so that we can correct our mistakes.

MASKS

NEED: A Halloween mask.
TEXT: Genesis 3:8.
POINT: We never need to hide from God. We can always trust in His love.

Would you like to be surprised today? All right, everyone close your eyes. Nobody peek. *(Put on the mask.)* You can open your eyes now. Did I scare you? Do you recognize me? If you didn't know who I was, you wouldn't recognize me, would you? *(Take off the mask.)*

Why do people wear masks like this? Do you ever wear a mask like this? Some people wear masks to scare people. Sometimes they wear masks like this so people can't recognize them. If you were trying to hide from someone, you might wear this mask so that person couldn't tell who you were. People can use masks to hide behind, can't they?

Is it possible to hide from God? If we put on a mask, can He still tell who we are? Let me put my mask back on. Now, can God tell who I am? Does He know me? Sure, He still knows me, doesn't he? *(Take off the mask.)* He can see right through my mask. God always knows who we are, no matter what disguise we might try to wear.

Is there any place we can go in the whole world to hide from God? Could God find us in Alaska? Could He find us in Australia? What if we went to the North Pole, could He find us there? Yes, there isn't any place we can go that God isn't already there. We can't hide from God, can we?

When do we want to hide from God? Usually when we do something wrong and we don't want anyone to see us. We don't even want God to see us. That's how some people in the Bible felt, too. Did you know that Adam tried to hide from God? When he disobeyed God, he tried to hide so that God couldn't find him. Jonah tried to hide from God, too. Do you think God found Adam and Jonah? He sure did. Many people tried to hide from God, but He found every one of them, didn't He?

Does God want us to hide from Him? No! He doesn't want us to wear masks or to run away from Him. Instead, He wants us to go to Him if we have a problem or if we have done something wrong. He wants us to trust that He still loves us. Jesus tells us that God is like a loving father. He can forgive us because He loves us. When we do something wrong, we don't need to hide from God, but we can go to Him, our Father, and be forgiven.

Summary: It's silly to try to hide from God, isn't it? He can see right through our masks. Can we hide anywhere in the world where God can't find us? No! So instead of trying to hide from God, He wants us to trust Him completely. He wants us to turn to Him for love and forgiveness.

MICROPHONE

NEED: A microphone.
TEXT: Jeremiah 1:4-8.
POINT: When God wants us to know something, He often speaks to us through people.

What do you do when you want to get a message to someone far away? You might write a letter or call that person on the telephone. But suppose you wanted to say something to a large number of people. How would you talk to them? You could use what I have in my hand. You could talk to them with a microphone, couldn't you?

What does a microphone do? It amplifies your voice, making it louder, so it can be heard at a distance. We use a microphone to speak to large crowds so that everyone can easily hear what is said, even the people who are farthest away from us. Let me ask you another question:

When God wants to tell us something, how does He do it? Does He speak to us through a microphone? No, He does something even better. He speaks to us through people like you and me. People are like God's microphones. When

God wants to get a message to us, He uses people to deliver that message.

How does God use people to deliver His messages? The Bible tells us about many people whom God wanted to be His messengers. Jeremiah, even though he was still very young, was chosen to tell the people about God's will. God chose another person, Paul, to bring the news about Jesus to people all over the Roman Empire. And God also wants us to tell others the good news about Jesus. In that way, we can be His microphones and deliver God's messages to other people.

What do you have to do to make a microphone work? You have to plug it in, don't you? That's the way it is for us, too. To be God's microphones, we have to be plugged into the source of our power, God himself. He gives us the strength and the wisdom to be His messengers in the world. We have to know the Bible, God's message to the world. Let's try it right now. One of the first Christian messages the Bible tells us about was simply to tell others, "Jesus is Lord." Let's say that together into the microphone. *(Everyone say, "Jesus is Lord.")* I'll bet everyone here heard that message of good news about Jesus. Thank you for being God's messengers today.

Summary: When God wants to tell us a message, He doesn't have to use a microphone, does He? He wants you and me to be His microphones and spread the good news about Him. That way, God's words are amplified so that everyone can know about Him, just as everyone heard our words today through this microphone.

NEW YEAR'S RESOLUTIONS

NEED: A list of New Year's resolutions.
TEXT: Romans 5:8.
POINT: Even though we should always try to do what God wants us to, we can still trust Him to forgive us when we make a mistake.

Who can see what I brought with me today. It is a piece of paper with a list of things on it. I have made a list of *resolutions*. Does anyone know what a resolution is? It is like a promise to myself. These are the things I promise to do or promise not to do in the future. Sometimes people make these promises when a new year begins; so they are often called New Year's resolutions.

What are some promises you might make to yourself on your list of resolutions? You might promise to help more around the house. You might promise not to fight with your brothers and sisters. Or you might promise to do all your homework on time. These are all resolutions or promises to yourself.

Do you think people always keep their resolutions? No,

sometimes we don't keep our promises to ourselves, do we? We promise we will be home in time for supper, but then we forget and come home late. We may want to like everyone, but then someone makes us angry. Jesus said that "the spirit is willing, but the flesh is weak" *(Mark 14:38)*. That means that we want to do the right thing, but we're not always able to do it. We don't always keep our resolutions.

Does God care whether or not we do what He want us to do? Yes, He wants very much for us to do the right thing. He has a plan for us, and He wants us to fulfill that plan and be all that He made us to be. But sometimes we fall short, and we don't always do His will. Even though God never breaks His promises to us, sometimes we break our promises to Him. What does God do when we break our resolutions to Him?

Does God turn His back on us when we fail? Does God say, "You made a mistake and failed to keep your promise; so I'm never going to have anything to do with you again"? No, He doesn't. God loves us so much that even when we make mistakes and break our promises, He comes to us. Paul says that God sent His Son, Jesus, to us while we were yet sinners, to save us from our sin. Even though we are not as good as we should be, God does not forget His promise to us. He still forgives us. He still loves us. And He still promises we will live with Him forever. Even though we don't, God always keeps His resolutions.

Summary: Whenever you make a promise to yourself, think about God's promise to you. I hope you will try your best to keep all your promises to God. But if you make a mistake, it's good to know that you can turn to God and be forgiven. Even though we sometimes fail, God's love and forgiveness never do.

NO PARKING

NEED: Two signs, "No Parking" and "Office," and a sign that says, "JESUS."

TEXT: John 6:26.

POINT: God is here all the time, even though we don't see Him.

How many of you know how to read? Then you can read what I brought with me today. Who can read what this says? *(Hold up the "No Parking" sign.)* Where do you see signs like this? What would happen if I didn't see this sign and parked my car in the wrong place? I might get a ticket or even have my car towed away. Signs can be important, can't they?

What does this sign say? *("Office.")* If you were looking for the lounge or your Sunday School room, would you follow this sign? No. You'd end up in the wrong place if you did. It is important to read signs and follow them, isn't it? There is another very important sign I want to tell you about today. *(Hold up the "Jesus" sign.)*

Who can tell me what this sign says? Did you know that

Jesus is God's sign to us? When Jesus came, the people were looking for something special. They were looking for a Savior, or a Messiah. They wanted someone who could bring forgiveness and give them new life. Is that what Jesus did? Yes, that's the reason we call Him our Savior. But not everyone understood this.

If you couldn't read, could you understand this sign? No, of course not. Many people did not understand that Jesus was God's sign to us, promising us forgiveness and new life. Jesus said that these people did not see God's sign in Moses or the prophets God sent; so it was no wonder that they didn't understand Jesus, either. They were still asking for a sign even after God had sent His Son, Jesus, to them as a sign of His love. It was as if they couldn't read.

Have you ever been lost? Maybe you've been riding in a strange town and lost your way. What do you do when you are lost? You probably look around for street signs and highway signs, don't you? The signs can tell you where you are and where you are going. That's a time when it is important to find the right sign. God wants us to see the sign He gives us, too. *(Hold up the "Jesus" sign again.)* Jesus is a sign to us of God's love.

Summary: The next time you see a sign, remember God has a sign for us, too. That sign is Jesus, and we read about Him in the Bible. God wants us to follow Him, even though many people didn't understand Him at the time. They were still asking for a sign. But when we get to know Jesus, we know that He is a sign to us, a sign of God's love.

PART OF A RECIPE

NEED: A recipe.
TEXT: Ecclesiastes 3:11.
POINT: Each of us is an important part of God's whole plan of creation.

How many of you like to help in the kitchen? Have you ever helped bake a cake or make cookies? It's fun to help in the kitchen, isn't it? If your mom was going to bake a cake, what would she need to get started? She might need some flour, some eggs, or some sugar. Those are some of the ingredients needed to make a cake.

But how does she know how much of each ingredient to use? She probably uses one of these. *(Show the recipe.)* Do you all know what a recipe is? It tells you exactly how much of everything you need to make a cake. For example, does it make any difference whether you use five cups of sugar or only two cups? It could make quite a difference in what the cake tastes like, couldn't it? Or suppose you put in only one egg instead of two. That would also change the taste of the cake. It's important to have a recipe when

39

you make a cake, isn't it? A recipe is important for another reason, too.

What would happen if you completely left out one of the ingredients? What if you forgot to put in the flour or the eggs? The cake wouldn't turn out very well, would it? A recipe helps you to remember everything you need to use. It is like a plan to help you make your cake. The Bible tells us about a different kind of recipe. It is God's creation. Like our cake, everything God made in this world is according to His plan.

Do you think that God made everything according to a plan? The Bible says that He did. He had a purpose in mind when He made the world and everything in it, including you and me. He made it all according to His plan, just as we make a cake by following a recipe. Everything He made was part of His plan.

Would the world be the same if God had left some things out? Suppose He had forgotten to make trees, or fish, or birds. The world would be different, wouldn't it? Suppose He would have forgotten you or me. The world would not be quite the same because we are all part of His plan. Do you think we are important to God? He tells us in the Bible that we are. He says we are all His children, and that each one of us is part of His plan. Just as every ingredient is important to make a cake, each one of us is an important part of God's creation.

Summary: The next time you help to make something in the kitchen, don't forget to follow a recipe. A recipe keeps you from forgetting an important ingredient that you need. In the same way, we are important ingredients in God's recipe for the world. We are all very important to God's plan, and He loves each one of us very much.

PEOPLE OR MONEY?

NEED: Two boxes, one with a dollar bill and a check for a million dollars, and the other with a family picture and a picture of Jesus.

TEXT: Matthew 6:24.

POINT: God wants us to serve one another and to put the needs of people ahead of accumulating possessions.

What do I have with me today? *(Two boxes.)* I'm going to ask you to choose which box you would rather have. First, I'll show you what is in this box. *(Show the dollar bill from the first box.)* This is a one-dollar bill, isn't it? Now what do I have in this other box? *(Show the family picture.)* It is a picture of my family. Let's pretend it is the people in your family, too. Now you have to decide:

Which would you rather have, the dollar or your family? Our families are much more important to us than a dollar, aren't they? But let me show you what else is in this first box. *(Hold up the check.)* I have here a check for one million dollars! Does that change your mind? Now which would you rather have, your family or a million dollars?

41

You'd still rather have your family, wouldn't you? If you had a million dollars, you couldn't replace your family. They are more important than money.

Can you think of anything you can't buy with money? Can you buy friendship with money? No, a real friend is your friend no matter how much money you have. Can you buy forgiveness with money? No, God forgives us because He loves us, not because of how much money we have. Is there any amount of money that can buy God's love? No, we can't buy God's love, can we? There is nothing wrong with money itself, but money can't buy the most important things in life. There is one more thing in this second box. *(Show the picture of Jesus.)* Whose picture is this?

Is Jesus more important than a million dollars? If we had a million dollars, could we buy what Jesus did for us? No, of course not. And Jesus taught that people are worth more than any amount of money in the world. He even gave His life for people like you and me. That's the reason He told His disciples that they should serve one another, because nothing is more important than people, not even all the money in the world.

Summary: Which box is more valuable? Even with all this money, you couldn't buy a new family. Jesus tells us that there are things money can't buy. People are more valuable than money.

PRACTICE DOESN'T MAKE PERFECT

NEED: A baseball and bat.
TEXT: Romans 3:21-26.
POINT: We don't become perfect through our own efforts, but through the righteousness of God in Jesus Christ.

How many of you have played baseball? Then I'm sure you know what these are. *(Show the baseball and bat.)* What do you try to do with this baseball bat? Then what do you do after you hit the ball? You try to run around all the bases and score a run for your team, don't you?

What is it called when you hit the ball so far that you get around all the bases without stopping? *(A home run.)* Is it easy to hit a home run? No, you have to hit the ball on the good wood of the bat just right *(hold the ball to the bat)* to hit it that far, don't you? If your swing is off even a little bit, you will hit a pop-up or a ground ball. It's much easier to make an out than to hit a home run, isn't it?

Does it take a lot of practice to be a good hitter? Yes, it takes practice to develop your coordination and timing and strength so that you can hit a home run. Have you ever gone to a baseball game early and watched the players take batting practice? Big leaguers have been playing baseball for many years, but even they still have to practice their hitting, don't they?

Do you think if you practiced long enough, you could hit a home run every time? Do you think you could ever become perfect? No one can hit a home run every time at bat. No matter how much you practice, you could never become perfect. It would be nice if you could go to bat and never make an out. It would be even better if you could go through life and never make a mistake. But we all make mistakes, don't we?

What does the Bible mean when it says we should be righteous? God wants us to do His will and do what is right. But sometimes we don't do the right thing, do we? It's like going to bat and making an out. Even though we try our best, sometimes that isn't good enough. But the Bible tells us that God loves us so much that He sent His Son, Jesus, so that we can be given *His* righteousness. We are perfect in Him instead of in ourselves.

When we make an out in a baseball game, does the coach kick us off the team? No, of course not. The coach knows that no one is perfect. God knows that no one is perfect, too. He knows that we need His righteousness because we cannot be righteous enough through our own efforts no matter how hard we try. Just as no one can hit a home run every time at bat, we cannot be perfect on our own. So we rely on God's righteousness. It is His righteousness that makes us perfect.

Summary: Think about all the practice it takes to become a good hitter. But no baseball player is perfect. None of us is perfect through our own efforts, either. It is God's righteousness, through Jesus, that makes us perfect in His sight.

TICKET TO THE
MAGIC KINGDOM

NEED: A couple of tickets, preferably tickets to an amusement park.

TEXT: Luke 23:42, 43.

POINT: Jesus wants us to be participants in the kingdom of God.

Can you see what I brought with me today? *(Show the tickets.)* What do you need tickets for? You might need a ticket to get into a movie, a ball game, or an amusement park. How many of you like to go to an amusement park? What do you like to do there? Do you like to go on the rides, go into the funhouse, and eat in the restaurants?

What would happen if you weren't allowed to do any of those things? Suppose you bought your ticket to the amusement park, but when you got there, you had to sit on a bench. Suppose you weren't allowed to eat anything or go on any of the rides. Would you ever go back to that park again? I wouldn't, either. It's not much fun just to sit and watch at an amusement park.

Have any of you ever been to *Disney World* **or the** *Magic Kingdom?* There are a lot of things to do, aren't there? Today I want to tell you about another kingdom that has a lot to do. The Bible calls it the kingdom of God. It is a special kingdom where God is the King, and we are all invited to be part of it. In it, we can enjoy all the gifts God wants to give us, now and forever. It is a very good place to live, even better than an amusement park.

How do you think you get into this kingdom of God? Do you need a ticket like these? No, you need a special ticket. That ticket is Jesus. Jesus invites us all to be in this special kingdom. He wants us all to be part of God's kingdom because He loves us, and He wants us to know the joy of being God's people. That's the reason Jesus is like a ticket into the kingdom of God. We get in through His forgiving love.

How much do you think it costs to get into God's kingdom? That's the best news of all. It's free. Jesus has already paid the price of the ticket. The kingdom is a free gift of God's grace, given to us because He loves us. But He doesn't want us just to sit and watch. He wants us to enjoy His gifts, care for His people, and help people when they need us. It's like going to an amusement park. You don't just sit around and do nothing. You participate. God wants us to be busy and active in His kingdom, too.

Summary: The next time you go to an amusement park, I hope you don't just sit on a bench and watch everyone else go on the rides. Just like this ticket to an amusement park, Jesus invites us into a very special kingdom called the kingdom of God. And in God's kingdom, He doesn't want us just to sit and watch, either.

Scripture Index

Object Talk Books

21 Object Talks for Teaching Children, by Larry R. Michaels (2891)

Bible Object Talks for Children, by Larry R. Michaels (2888)

Teaching with Object Talks, by Cara Roberts (2889)

Object Talks on the Parables of Jesus, by Lois Edstrom (2857)

Object Talks on the Teachings of Jesus (2858)

Object Talks for Special Days (2859)

Object Talks on Christian Living (2860)